AQA

Self Study Guide

Clare Parker

OXFORD

UNIVERSITY PRESS

OXFORD
UNIVERSITY PRESS

Great Clarendon Street, Oxford OX2 6DP

Oxford University Press is a department of the University of Oxford.
It furthers the University's objective of excellence in research, scholarship,
and education by publishing worldwide in

Oxford   New York
Auckland   Cape Town   Dar es Salaam   Hong Kong   Karachi
Kuala Lumpur   Madrid   Melbourne   Mexico City   Nairobi
New Delhi   Shanghai   Taipei   Toronto

With offices in

Argentina   Austria   Brazil   Chile   Czech Republic   France   Greece
Guatemala   Hungary   Italy   Japan   South Korea   Poland   Portugal
Singapore   Switzerland   Thailand   Turkey   Ukraine   Vietnam

Oxford is a registered trade mark of Oxford University Press
in the UK and in certain other countries

British Library Cataloguing in Publication Data

Data available

ISBN 978 019 915373 2

3 5 7 9 10 8 6 4 2

Typeset by Thomson

Printed in Great Britain by Ashford Colour Press Ltd.

Acknowledgements

The author and publisher would like to thank Melissa Weir (project
manager) and Marion Dill (language consultant).

Contents

General Exam Tips

Here's a reminder of the topics you have studied for AS Level and which you now need to revise.

Media

▶ Television
▶ Advertising
▶ Communication Technology

Popular Culture

▶ Cinema
▶ Music
▶ Fashion/Trends

Healthy Living/Lifestyle

▶ Sport/Exercise
▶ Health and well-being
▶ Holidays

Family/Relationships

▶ Relationships within the family
▶ Friendships
▶ Marriage/Partnerships

You will be taking two examinations:

Unit 1: Listening, Reading and Writing

This paper is worth **70%** of your AS Level (and **35% of the full A** Level) and the time allowed is two hours.

There are three sections:

▶ Listening and Reading
▶ Reading and Writing
▶ Writing

Acc. No.

00407046

Class No.

438 PAR

Unit 2: Speaking Test

The Speaking Test is worth **30%** of your AS grade (and **15%** of the full A Level).
The test lasts 15 minutes and you have 20 minutes to prepare beforehand.
You are not allowed to use a dictionary.

There are two sections:

▶ Discussing a stimulus card
▶ General conversation on topics you have studied.

**Pass grades for this examination range from A down to E.
Here's an idea of what you need to be able to do.**

If you pass AS Level German with an A grade, it means you can:

▶ Clearly understand spoken language, including details and people's opinions.

▶ Work out what someone is trying to say even if they don't spell it out in detail.

▶ Clearly understand written texts, understanding both the gist and the details.

▶ Talk fluently, giving your opinions and justifying them, and using a good range of vocabulary and generally accurate pronunciation.

▶ Organise your ideas and write them up well in German.

▶ Write using a wide range of vocabulary and grammatical structures without making many mistakes.

If you pass AS Level German with an E grade, it means you:

▶ Show some understanding of spoken German, even if you have difficulties when the language is complex and miss some of the details.

▶ Can sometimes work out what someone is trying to say even if they don't give all the details.

▶ Understand straightforward written texts, although you don't always understand more difficult writing.

▶ Can talk in German, and convey basic information, perhaps a little hesitantly and relying on material you have learned by heart. There is probably some English influence on your pronunciation.

▶ Can convey information in writing, perhaps with some difficulty in organising your material and expressing it.

▶ Use a range of vocabulary and structures, but quite often you make mistakes.

Preparing for the exams

You can see from these lists that when planning your revision there are really six areas you need to practise:

▶ Speaking

▶ Listening

▶ Reading

▶ Writing

▶ Vocabulary

▶ Grammar

There are tips on how to prepare each area overleaf.

Speaking

▶ Take every opportunity to practise speaking German – in lessons, with the language assistant, with a friend, with anyone you know who speaks German.

▶ Take an oral question from your textbook and work out a few sentences to answer it, then record them on tape and listen to see what areas still need practice – perhaps fluency, pronunciation or good use of vocabulary and structures.

▶ Don't write everything down first. You won't have a script on the day! You can write a few key words down for reference, but definitely no full sentences.

Listening

▶ Keep listening to German, ideally every day. Use a mix of extracts you have worked on and new texts.

▶ Try listening to something for which you have the transcript. Just listen first, then listen again with the transcript and, if necessary, look up unknown words. Finally, listen again without the transcript and challenge yourself to understand everything.

▶ Watching films is excellent listening practice and watching more than once is even better! Try watching with the subtitles and then without. If you find this hard going, just re-watch a short extract.

▶ German radio and TV programmes are useful, but can also be difficult. Record an extract and listen or watch it more than once. You will find it gets easier.

▶ Make sure you do some exam listening practice too!

Reading

▶ Keep reading a mix of things you read once quickly, such as a magazine, and things where you work hard at a short passage and try to understand everything. Texts from your textbook are useful for this.

▶ It's useful to note new vocabulary from your reading, but don't make it such hard work that you give up. Note, say, three new words from each text.

▶ Try a 'dual-language' reading book, where you get the original German on one page and an English translation on the opposite one. This is an excellent way to practise reading longer texts without losing heart!

▶ Search on the internet for articles in German on any topic which interests you.

Writing

▶ Practise planning essay questions. Jot down ideas for each paragraph – in German! – along with key vocabulary.

▶ Take a key paragraph from a piece of marked work, write some English prompts to remind you of its content and then write it out from memory. Concentrate especially on sections where the teacher suggested improvements.

▶ Look carefully at marked work and identify what grammar errors you are making. Then check them up in a grammar book and try some practice exercises.

▶ Make sure you are learning key vocabulary for each topic area, so that whichever subject comes up you will have some impressive words to use.

Vocabulary

▶ Learn lists of words regularly and build in time to go back over words you learned a week or two ago. Reinforcement makes them stick!

▶ Choose a system of recording new words which works for you. It could be paper lists, small sections on individual cards, recording the words and their English meanings on tape, making posters to stick on your bedroom wall ... what's important is that you are noting the words and going over them regularly!

▶ You were probably encouraged to use a good range of vocabulary in the essays you wrote during the year. Go back over them, highlighting good words and phrases and writing the English in the margin, then use this to test yourself. Words are often easier to learn in context.

Grammar

▶ Keep doing practice exercises in areas where you know you are weak.

▶ Use reading texts to practise thinking grammatically. For example, highlight a selection of adjectives, then write out the English for the phrases in which they appear. Test yourself by reproducing the German phrases accurately, complete with all the correct agreements!

▶ Keep learning from your verb tables until you know all the forms of each tense of regular verbs and the most common irregular verbs. Test yourself using a die. 1 = *ich*, 2 = *du*, 3 = *er*/*sie*/*es*, 4 = *wir*, 5 = *ihr*, 6 = *Sie*/*sie*. Use a verb list: choose an infinitive and a tense at random, throw the die and say the correct form of the verb. Practise until you can do it without hesitation.

The Speaking Test: what you need to know

The test has two parts: discussing a stimulus card and conversation on the topics you have studied.

Discussing a stimulus card (five minutes)

▶ Choose one of the two cards you are given and spend the preparation time on it.

▶ Prepare an answer of two or three sentences for the first question, which is usually, 'Worum handelt es?' or 'Worum geht es?'

▶ The other questions often ask for reasons, opinions, ideas for or against something. Think widely and come up with two or three ideas, not just one!

▶ The conversation will move onto broader issues, which will be linked to the topic. Try to imagine what else you could be asked and think what answer you would give.

▶ You are allowed to make notes. Don't write out exactly what you will say, but do note some useful vocabulary for the topic.

To do well on this section you need to have a wide range of ideas and to develop them, by giving your opinions, your own ideas, reasons and examples. Your knowledge of grammar is also important – try to use some of the vocabulary and structures you have learned during the AS course, but stick to those you feel you can use fairly accurately.

Conversation on the topics you have studied (10 minutes)

This will be on three of the four topics you have studied:

Media

Popular Culture

Healthy Living and Lifestyle

Family and Relationships

You can choose the first topic. None of the topics will overlap with the material from the stimulus card. You will be asked questions on various aspects of the topic and the examiner will pick up on the things you say and ask you to explain or develop them further. So, be careful to mention only things you are happy to discuss further!

This section is marked on four aspects:

▶ **fluency,** which means speaking at a reasonable speed, although you may need time to think between utterances.

▶ **interaction,** i.e. answering what you are asked, but also taking the lead sometimes and giving more details.

▶ **pronunciation and intonation,** which really means sounding as 'German' as possible.

▶ **grammar** – see the notes above.

Family/relationships

> *Heutzutage ist es wahr, dass Familien nicht mehr sehr viel zusammen machen. Die Kinder haben oft andere Ideen und einsamere Freizeitsbeschäftigungen als ihre Eltern.*

Questions

Worum geht es hier?

Warum machen Familien so wenig zusammen?

Wie wichtig ist Kommunikation in Familien?

Was sind heute die anderen Probleme für Familien?

Welche Gefahren ergeben sich aus den neuen Technologien für Familien?

Prepare detailed answers to the questions. Look at these answers. They get better as they get fuller and more detailed:

▶ *Es geht um Familien.*

▶ *Es handelt sich um Kinder, die andere Freizeitsbeschäftigungen als ihre Eltern haben.*

▶ *Es geht hier um die Kommunikation zwischen Eltern und Jugendlichen und den Einfluss der modernen Technologie auf die verschiedenen Generationen. Die Eltern mögen lieber fernsehen, während die Jugendlichen lieber einsamere Freizeitsbeschäftigungen wie Computerspiele haben. Ich finde das ziemlich typisch für das heutige Familienleben.*

Role of parents/importance of good parenting

> Ich arbeite bei einer Familie. Ich kümmere mich den ganzen Tag um den kleinen Hans. Meine Arbeitgeber sind beide Geschäftsführer. Sie arbeiten den ganzen Tag bis ziemlich spät und sind fast nie zu Hause während der Woche.

Questions

Worum geht es hier?

Wie sehen Sie das Leben des kleinen Hans?

Was für Probleme gibt es für Kinder wie Hans, dessen Eltern sehr beschäftigt sind?

Was sind die anderen Schwierigkeiten im Leben einer Familie in der heutigen Gesellschaft?

Meinen Sie, dass Familie wichtiger als Freunde sein sollte?

The last four questions ask you to think of ideas and opinions. To answer such questions, you need to have about three ideas ready. For example, to answer the third question, you could say:

Ein Kind so wie Hans, das nicht sehr viel Zeit mit seinen Eltern verbringt, könnte wenig Selbstvertrauen haben. Es ist möglich, dass er glaubt, er sei nicht sehr wichtig im Leben seiner Eltern. Ich meine, dass er oft sehr allein und einsam ist und dass er später im Leben Probleme mit seinen Eltern und mit seinen eigenen Kindern haben wird.

Read and listen to this student's answers to the five questions from Speaking Test 2.

CD Track 1

Worum geht es hier?

Es geht hier um den kleinen Hans, der nicht sehr viel Zeit mit seinen Eltern verbringt, weil sie sehr viel arbeiten und sehr beschäftigt sind. Ein junges Mädchen kümmert sich den ganzen Tag um ihn.

Wie sehen Sie das Leben des kleinen Hans?

Ich glaube, dass der Hans sehr einsam sein muss. Vielleicht sieht er seine Eltern ganz kurz am Morgen, bevor sie zur Arbeit gehen, und wenn sie nach Hause kommen, ist er schon im Bett. Er wird mehr Zeit mit seinen Eltern am Wochenende verbringen.

Was für Probleme gibt es für Kinder wie Hans, dessen Eltern sehr beschäftigt sind?

Sicher fehlen ihm seine Eltern viel, und er würde sie lieber öfter sehen. Vielleicht ist er unglücklich. Das Verhältnis zwischen ihm und seinen Eltern muss auch schwierig sein, da sie nicht sehr viel zusammen machen.

Was sind die anderen Schwierigkeiten im Leben einer Familie in der heutigen Gesellschaft?

Es gibt heutzutage sicher Geldprobleme, da Häuser sehr viel Geld kosten. Wenn Eltern arbeitslos sind, gibt es auch finanzielle Schwierigkeiten. Dann gibt es Generationsprobleme, wenn die Eltern nicht verstehen, was die Kinder machen wollen. Es gibt immer verschiedene Meinungen zu Themen wie Sex.

Meinen Sie, dass Familie wichtiger als Freunde sein sollte?

Es kommt darauf an. Für mich, nein, da meine Eltern geschieden sind. Meine Eltern müssen sehr viel arbeiten und haben wenig Zeit für mich. Sie verstehen mich überhaupt nicht, und ich finde, dass meine Freunde immer für mich da sind.

Now the examiner may ask other questions on the same general topic area. Here are some examples:

- Was sind die Vorteile für ein Einzelkind wie Hans? Und die Nachteile?
- Welche Rolle spielen die Großeltern im Leben einer modernen Familie?
- Wie sehen Sie das Familienleben in der Zukunft?

The conversation on topics you have studied

You will be asked questions on three of the four topic areas. These pages suggest sample questions for each section. Practise answering them, then try thinking up more questions of your own for each section. That's a good way to revise the material you have covered and to try and predict what you might be asked.

Media

- Meinen Sie, dass Sie zu viel Zeit vor dem Fernseher verbringen?
- Welche Sendungen sehen Sie lieber?
- Wie finden Sie Realitätssendungen wie ‚Big Brother'?
- Gibt es genug Sendungen für ältere Leute?
- Gibt es heutzutage zu viel Werbung?
- Sollte man Werbung für Alkohol und Tabak verbieten?
- Was wären die Nachteile, wenn es keine Werbung mehr gäbe?
- Ist es nötig, dass jeder ein Handy besitzt?
- Finden Sie, dass man genug Sicherheit im Internet hat?
- Wie alt sollte man sein, um das Internet zu benutzen?

If you make a general statement, back it up with examples. For example, if you are discussing celebrities, you might say that „berühmte Leute sollten Vorbilder für andere Leute sein." This has more weight if you follow it up by saying „zum Beispiel mag ich David Beckham gern, weil er versucht, jungen Leuten im Sport zu helfen."

Popular Culture

- Ist es wahr, dass nur die Filme, in denen viel Geld steckt, erfolgreich sein können?
- Meinen Sie, dass junge Leute sich mehr für Kino als für Bücher interessieren?
- Gehen Sie lieber ins Kino oder sehen Sie sich lieber eine DVD an?
- Erzählen Sie mir etwas über einen guten Film, den Sie neulich gesehen haben!
- Welche Musik hören Sie gern und warum?
- Wie sehen Sie die Musik der Zukunft?
- Müssen Sie die gleiche Musik wie Ihre Freunde mögen?
- Ist Ihre Kleidung ein Teil Ihrer Persönlichkeit?
- Wie hat sich die Freizeit seit der Jugend Ihrer Eltern geändert?
- Erzählen Sie mir etwas von einer berühmten Person, die Sie bewundern!

Healthy Living and Lifestyle

- Finden Sie, dass traditionelle Sportarten heutzutage altmodisch sind?
- Warum sollte man Sport treiben?
- Macht man in Ihrer Schule genug Sport?
- Wie kann man fit bleiben, wenn man keinen Sport mag?
- Was ist die schlimmste Gefahr für junge Leute – Alkohol, Tabak oder Drogen?
- Was heißt für Sie ‚sich gesund ernähren'?
- Welche täglichen Aktivitäten sind für die Gesundheit am gefährlichsten?
- Wie wichtig ist Urlaub für Sie?
- Was sind die Nachteile von Tourismus?
- Was kann man während den Ferien außer Reisen machen?

Remember that the examiner will respond to what you say, so be careful to introduce ideas you are happy to talk about! Here are three possible ways to begin answering the same question:

‚Wie wichtig ist Urlaub für Sie?'

▶ *Für mich ist Urlaub wichtig, um täglichen Stress zu vermeiden. Zum Beispiel …*

▶ *Was mir wichtig ist, ist Zeit mit Freunden zu verbringen. Ich mag am liebsten …*

▶ *Ich mag Urlaub, wo man die Umwelt respektieren kann. Daher mag ich lieber zelten und …*

Family and Relationships

- Welche Rolle spielen die Eltern im Leben eines jungen Menschen von 17 oder 18 Jahren?
- Worüber streiten sich junge Leute und andere Familienmitglieder?
- Was wäre Ihnen lieber, Einzelkind zu sein oder Geschwister zu haben?
- Wie sieht für Sie die ideale Familie aus?
- Was ist Ihnen wichtiger, Freunde oder Familie?
- Streiten Sie sich mit Freunden? Worüber?
- Was ist für Sie ein guter Freund?
- Wie wichtig ist heutzutage die Ehe?
- Wie kann man die Auswirkungen auf Kinder verringern, wenn die Eltern sich scheiden lassen?
- Was sind die Vorteile davon, ledig zu bleiben?

Take the lead in discussion on occasions. If the examiner makes a point you don't agree with, don't be afraid to say so! For example, suppose you are discussing the benefits and drawbacks of staying single and the examiner says: „Man hat aber viel mehr Freiheit, wenn man ledig bleibt." You could reply: „Es gibt aber auch Nachteile. Man fühlt sich von Zeit zur Zeit sehr einsam, und man hat nicht immer jemanden da, wenn man Probleme diskutieren möchte."

The Listening, Reading and Writing Paper

You can plan your time as you wish, but there are suggested amounts of time to spend on each section.

Listening and Reading (35 marks)

Suggested time: 30 minutes

There will be about five minutes of recording altogether and you will be able to play it and pause it yourself. There will be one passage with English questions on it and two to four more passages with other types of question in German, for example:

▶ reading statements and deciding which speaker said those things

▶ matching sentence halves

▶ multiple choice questions.

Reading and Writing (40 marks)

Suggested time: 45 minutes

There will be three or four passages of German to read, with a variety of types of question, for example:

▶ marking statements true/false/not mentioned or positive/negative/both

▶ deciding which of a list of statements summarises a particular person's viewpoint

▶ answering questions in German

▶ filling words from a box into gaps in a text.

In addition there will be a grammar test, where gapped sentences are given with a suggested verb, noun or adjective to fill the gaps. You will have to decide which form of the word to use.

Writing (35 marks)

Suggested time: 45 minutes

There will be a choice of three questions and you have to write one piece of at least 200 words. The questions vary and you could be asked to write in various formats, such as a letter, an article, an essay or a report. All the titles are based on topics from the syllabus.

The key ways to prepare are by:

▶ learning key vocabulary for each topic area

▶ revising the main grammar points

▶ doing plenty of listening practice to keep your ear 'tuned in' to German

▶ practising writing 200 word pieces in about 45 minutes

▶ working through the exam-type questions and tips on the following pages.

Familie

Transcript 1, CD Track 2

Answer the following questions in English.

1. What is Vanessa's family situation?

_____

_____

_____

2. What does her mother think she ought to do?

_____

_____

3. What problem does Lukas have?

_____

_____

4. How does he describe his mother?

_____

_____

5. Describe Donata's problem!

_____

_____

6. What effect has this problem on her life?

_____

_____

> Read questions carefully. Pay attention to marks given for each question as this is indicative of the amount of detail required.

Drei Jugendliche sprechen über ihre Familienprobleme.

Vanessa: Meine Eltern sind seit zwölf Jahren geschieden, und ich wohne mit meiner Mutter und meinem Bruder zusammen. Mein Vater hat jahrelang keinen Kontakt mit uns gehabt, aber plötzlich will er uns wieder sehen. Ich habe keine Lust, ihn kennen zu lernen, aber mein Bruder will sich mit ihm treffen. Meine Mutter meint, ich solle ihm eine Chance geben, aber es ist meine Entscheidung. Ich weiß nicht, was ich tun soll!

Lukas: Ich bin Einzelkind und vierzehn Jahre alt. Meine Mutter und ich streiten immer. Sie ist sehr ängstlich und behandelt mich wie ein kleines Kind. Sie ist immer misstrauisch und glaubt mir nie. Ich brauche mehr Selbstständigkeit, aber wie schaffe ich das mit meiner Mutter?

Donata: Ich bin die zweitälteste von vier Kindern. Meine ältere Schwester ist sehr sportlich und kriegt immer gute Noten in der Schule, ich leider nicht. Mein Vater ist von mir enttäuscht und kritisiert mich ständig vor der ganzen Familie. Er macht sich auch lustig über mich, auch vor Fremden. Ich habe nicht sehr viel Selbstvertrauen, und meine Noten in der Schule werden immer schlechter. Was soll ich machen?

Medien

Transcript 2, CD Track 3

Wer sagt was? Marianne (M), Peter (P) oder Jessica (J)? Schreiben Sie den entsprechenden Buchstaben ins Kästchen.

1. Werbung ist eine Art Manipulierung.

2. Werbung informiert uns über neue Produkte.

3. Eine freie Marktwirtschaft braucht Werbung.

4. Werbung ist unrealistisch.

5. Man sollte Werbung für bestimmte Produkte verbieten.

6. Man sollte prüfen, was in Werbespots gezeigt wird.

> Listen for synonyms – different ways of describing the same thing. Read statements very carefully.

Interviewer: Hallo von Jugend heute! Wir hören immer, dass es viel zu viel Werbung im Fernsehen, im Radio und auf den Straßen gibt. Die Frage: Sollte man alle Werbung verbieten? Wir haben drei Studenten aus Berlin nach ihrer Meinung gefragt.

Hallo, Marianne. Was können Sie zu diesem Thema sagen?

Marianne: Also, ich glaube, Werbung kann schon nützlich sein. Die Werbung informiert uns alle über neue Produkte und Sonderangebote. Teilweise gibt es aber zu viel Werbung, besonders die an Kinder gerichtete Werbung. Kinder sind sehr leicht zu beeinflussen, und das bereitet Probleme für die Eltern. Ich würde alle Werbung im Fernsehen verbieten, wenn Kindersendungen laufen.

Interviewer: Und Sie, Peter, was sagen Sie dazu?

Peter: Ohne Werbung gibt es Schwierigkeiten für Firmen, uns auf ihre Produkte aufmerksam zu machen. Da wir in einer Konsumgesellschaft leben, ist die Werbung unentbehrlich. Anstatt alle Werbung zu verbieten, würde ich lieber den Inhalt kontrollieren, um Stereotypen abzubauen.

Interviewer: Und zuletzt Jessica. Würden Sie Werbung verbieten?

Jessica: Ich würde sehr gern Werbung im Fernsehen verbieten. Werbung stört immer, wenn ich einen Film angucke. Ich möchte gern einmal in Ruhe fernsehen. Werbung kann auch sehr gefährlich sein, da sie ein ideales Weltbild darstellt und sehr verführerisch sein kann. Das ist nichts anderes als Gehirnwäsche, besonders für junge Leute.

Gesundes Leben

Transcript 3, CD Track 4

Wählen Sie die richtige Antwort.

1. Annike findet das Lernen

langweilig ⬜

stressig ⬜

einfach ⬜

2. Für Medizin braucht man

durchschnittliche Noten ⬜

niedrige Noten ⬜

sehr gute Noten ⬜

3. Annika entspannt sich

sehr oft ⬜

selten ⬜

nie ⬜

4. Sie isst gern

Fastfood ⬜

frische Lebensmittel ⬜

Schokolade ⬜

Read the question and possible answers very carefully. Listen to the item very carefully. Look out for negatives and 'false friends', which could mislead you.

Annike ist Studentin und wohnt in Freiburg. Sie macht nächstes Jahr ihr Abitur und möchte dann Medizin studieren.

Annike: Ich finde mein Leben ganz schön stressig. Ich stehe jeden Morgen sehr früh auf, um meine Hausaufgaben zu machen. Ich kann mich morgens viel besser konzentrieren. Ich stehe unter viel Stress, weil man für Medizin einen höheren Notendurchschnitt braucht als für andere Fächer. Ich glaube, dass es sehr wichtig ist, auf meine Gesundheit zu achten. Ich entspanne mich regelmäßig, um mich ausgeglichener zu fühlen und intensiver lernen zu können. Ich entspanne mich am besten mit Musik oder einem langen Bad. Ich achte darauf, dass ich genug Schlaf bekomme und dass ich gesund esse. Fastfood kann ich nicht leiden. Das ist zu fettig für mich. Ich esse lieber Salate und frisches Gemüse und trinke Fruchtsäfte.

Populäre Kultur

Transcript 4, CD Track 5

Beantworten Sie die folgenden Fragen auf Deutsch:

1. In welchem Bereich möchten Mädchen lieber arbeiten?

_____

2. Welche Kompetenzen werden Jungen und Mädchen in der künftigen Arbeitswelt brauchen?

_____

_____

3. Welche persönliche Eigenschaften brauchen sie auch?

_____

_____

Immer mehr Jungen wollen Fußballer werden. Mädchen träumen dagegen von einer Karriere als Ärztin. In einer Umfrage des Münchner Instituts für Jugendforschung erklärten 14,5% der Jungen, Kicker sei ihr Traumjob. Auf Platz zwei kam Polizist, gefolgt von Pilot und Kfz-Mechaniker. Bei Mädchen steht der Umfrage zufolge Helfen hoch im Kurs. Mehr als ein Viertel möchte Tierärztin, Ärztin oder Krankenschwester werden. Model oder Schauspielerin liegen bei den Berufswünschen der Mädchen erst hinter Polizistin oder Lehrerin. Zum ersten Mal tauchten Computerberufe auf der Liste von Jungen (4,1%) und Mädchen (1,0%) auf. Und welche Kompetenzen werden sie in der künftigen Arbeitswelt brauchen? Die meisten nannten eine gute Ausbildung, Computer- und Sprachkenntnisse als wichtige Eigenschaften – Kompetenzen, die auch in der Wunschliste von Geschäftsführern auftauchen. Die Umfrage nannte auch gute Kommunikationsfähigkeiten, Flexibilität und Teamfähigkeiten als wichtige persönliche Eigenschaften. Die Wirtschaft sucht außerdem Mitarbeiter, die fließend Englisch sprechen und eine gute Allgemeinbildung haben. „Bloß keine Fachidioten, die nichts anderes im Kopf haben", meinte der Direktor eines großen Kölner Medienhauses.

Familie

Text 1

Lesen Sie den folgenden Text:

Ehe in der Krise

Die Ehe ist tot. Das alte Modell von Ehe „bis dass der Tod uns scheidet"
ist heute sehr altmodisch geworden. Spaß miteinander ist heute das
Hauptmotiv für Gemeinsamkeit, und nach einigen Jahren finden die
Partner sich nicht mehr attraktiv. 50% aller Frauen würden ihren Mann
einige Jahre später nicht noch einmal heiraten. Für viele ist auch die
Karriere wichtiger als Beziehungen, und für manche ist der Computer
viel spannender als Sex. In früheren Jahrhunderten dauerten Ehen im
Schnitt etwa acht Jahre, weil dann oft die Frau im Kindbett starb. Heute
dauert eine Ehe, wenn sie nicht geschieden wird, durchschnittlich 43
Jahre. In der Zukunft könnte sie, da die Menschen immer länger leben, 60
bis 70 Jahren dauern. Es ist aber nicht unbedingt natürlich für Menschen,
auf Dauer zusammenzubleiben. Politiker planen jetzt neue Gesetze, um
Scheidung leichter und billiger zu machen. Ein Scheidungscomputer
könnte in der Zukunft die Scheidungsanwälte ersetzen.

Sind diese Sätze Richtig (R), Falsch (F) oder Nicht im Text (N/T)?

1. Die Ehe auf Lebenszeit ist nicht mehr aktuell.

2. Der Hauptgrund für Zusammenleben ist Liebe.

3. Jede zweite Ehefrau würde ihren Mann schon
   nach sechs Jahren wieder heiraten.

4. Die Scheidungsraten nehmen in Deutschland immer mehr ab.

5. Eine Ehe könnte in der Zukunft mehr als fünfzig Jahren dauern.

6. Neue Gesetze werden Scheidung schwieriger machen.

Read statements and text very carefully. Watch out for negatives and
synonyms and antonyms.

Gesundes Leben

Text 2

Lesen Sie den folgenden Text:

Stress, Herzkrankheiten, Abhängigkeiten von verschiedenen Drogen (Tabak, Alkohol usw.) Krebs – diese Krankheiten unserer Zeit kann man vermeiden. Man muss nur bereit sein, seinen ungesunden Lebensstil zu ändern.

Eine ausgeglichene Ernährung mit vielen Vitaminen kann den Cholesterinspiegel reduzieren und vor Herzinfarkt schützen.

Der moderne Mensch steht häufig unter Stress. Man füllt seine Tage mit immer mehr Aktivitäten, nimmt sich aber nicht mehr Zeit dafür. Entspannung, Yoga und Meditation können helfen, Stress abzubauen. Eine neue Art sich zu entspannen ist ‚Stopping'. Man bekommt praktische Ratschläge, wie man die Dinge erkennen kann, die wirklich wichtig sind.

Beantworten Sie die Fragen.

1. Wie kann man so genannte Zeitkrankheiten vermeiden?

   _____

2. Warum ist eine ausgeglichene Ernährung wichtig?

   _____

   _____

3. Warum gibt es so viel Stress im Leben?

   _____

4. Wie kann man den Druck reduzieren?

   _____

   _____

5. Wie funktioniert ‚Stopping'?

   _____

> Use the language of the questions and the text and reword the answers using your knowledge of German grammar.

Medien

Text 3

Lesen Sie den folgenden Text:

Hausaufgaben online!

Vor einem Jahr ging der 19-jährige Gymnasiast Bastian Wilhelm aus Celle mit seinem Hausaufgaben-Service online. www.cheat.ne.de bietet jede Menge Referate und Stoffsammlungen zu den verschiedensten Themen. Die Idee enstand vor etwa drei Jahren, als Bastian bei einem seiner ersten Surfs feststellen musste, dass es online kaum etwas Interessantes und Brauchbares für Schüler gab. Bei einem Austauschjahr in den USA lernte er zufällig einen Internet-Provider kennen, der ihm alles rund um Netz beibrachte. Auf diese Weise erkannte er, welche Möglichkeiten das Internet bieten konnte. Er musste dann Investoren suchen, damit er keine Miete zahlen musste. Die Seite hat inzwischen 7000 Besucher pro Tag.

Die Zeit spielt eine wichtige Rolle für Bastian. Er arbeitet täglich an seiner Internetseite, aber er sieht im Computer nur ein Mittel, um Zeit zu sparen.

Die Reaktionen auf sein cheat.net waren bisher hauptsächlich positiv. Sein Vater, der selbst Rektor ist, hält den Service für eine ,wunderbare' Recherchemöglichkeit. Wunderbar finden diese Projekte aber vor allem die Schüler.

Auf Deutsch heißt „cheat" zwar so viel wie Betrug oder Schwindel, doch das ist nicht die Grundidee der Seite. „Wer die Infos herunterlädt, ohne seinen Kopf einzusetzen und das Material nachzuprüfen, ist selbst Schuld", sagt Bastian. „Denn nicht alles, was im Internet steht, ist wahr."

Füllen Sie die Lücken mit der richtigen Form der Verben.

1. Die Idee für die Webseite _____ vor etwa drei Jahren.
   (entstehen)

2. Bastian _____ in Amerika einen Internet-Provider
   _____. (kennen lernen)

3. Er findet, dass er damit Zeit _____ könnte. (sparen)

4. Die Schüler _____ den Service wunderbar. (finden)

5. Es ist nicht gut, dass man die Infos einfach _____.
   (herunterladen)

6. Es ist sehr wichtig, dass man das Material _____.
   (nachprüfen)

Populäre Kultur

Text 4

Lesen Sie den folgenden Text und setzen Sie die fehlenden Wörter in die Lücken. Achten Sie dabei auf die Grammatik!

Hollywood. Die Krönung war triumphal. ‚Die Rückkehr des Königs‘, der letzte _____ der ‚Herr der Ringe‘-Triologie von Peter Jackson, war beinah alleinherrisch bei der 76. Oscarvergabe in Hollywood. In elf _____ war der monumentale Film nominiert, in allen hat er _____ und ist als erster Fantasy-Film überhaupt zur besten Produktion des Jahres gekürt worden. „Ich _____ das noch gar nicht glauben. Der Sturm heute Abend war mehr, als wir _____ hatten", sagt der 42-jährige Neuseeländer Jackson, erschöpft und glücklich nach der Gala im Kodak-Theater. Die Verfilmung des großen Romans von J. R. R. Tolkien „war das Härteste, was ich je in meinem Leben gemacht habe. Es hat mich fast umgebracht – aber jetzt ist es gut." Gut bis auf die Schuhe, die sich der Barfußläufer Jackson für den Gang über den roten Teppich angezogen hatte. „Meine _____ schmerzen wie die Hölle."

Fuß	abräumen	Kategorie
berühmt	Stars	erwarten
Teil	können	warten

Use knowledge of grammar to help you, e.g. gap 1 is obviously a masculine singular noun. Gap 3 is obviously a past participle of a verb. Then use elimination and the sense of the sentence to help you to work out the missing word.

Writing: sample questions

> Schreiben Sie einen Artikel für eine Jugendzeitschrift, in dem Sie Ihre Einstellung zu den heutigen Problemen in Familien darstellen. Was kann man machen, um die Situation in vielen Familien leichter zu machen?

> Rauchverbot in der Öffentlichkeit – ja oder nein?

> "Durch Filme und Fernsehsendungen sehen wir Gewalt nicht mehr als einen Ausnahmezustand, sondern als einen normalen Zustand, der zu wachsender Kriminalität unter jungen Menschen führt. Filme, die Gewalt verherrlichen, sollten nicht im Fernsehen gezeigt werden."
>
> "Gewalt ist eine Tatsache in der heutigen Gesellschaft. Es ware also unrealistisch, sie ganz aus dem Fernsehen zu verbannen. Vielleicht könnte man den Inhalt besser prüfen, damit Gewalt nicht verherrlicht wird, sondern aus der Opferperspektive gezeigt wird."
>
> Wie finden Sie diese Meinungen? Sollen wir Gewaltfilme am Fernsehen verbieten? Schreiben Sie einen Brief an eine Zeitung, in dem Sie Ihre Meinung äußern.

> Mode: Wie wichtig ist Mode in Ihrem Leben?

Writing tips

When attempting any of these questions, ensure that you read them carefully and pay as much attention to the question itself as to the stimulus material. You need to decide very quickly which question you are going to answer.

Make a plan with a beginning, a middle and an end. Deal with both sides of the argument, if appropriate, and make sure that you add your own opinion, justified with examples.

Make sure your sentences link well, using conjunctions and relative clauses and a range of tenses. Use the first person when requested to do so and write at least 200 words.

Build in enough time to check your work carefully. Read through looking for specific things i.e. the first time just the verbs, checking tenses, agreements and positions; read through the second time looking at nouns and adjectives, agreements and capital letters.

Your essay will be marked for Content, Vocabulary, Structure and Accuracy. The range used is as follows. Remember that the marks awarded for vocabulary, structure and accuracy cannot be more than one band higher than the mark awarded for content.

	Content	Vocabulary	Structure	Accuracy
V. good	17–20	5	5	5
Good	13–16	4	4	4
Sufficient	9–12	3	3	3
Limited	5–8	2	2	2
Poor	1–4	1	1	1
Not relevant	0	0	0	0

Grammar Summary

1 Nouns and articles

1.1 Gender

Every German noun has a gender. There are some patterns which make learning correct genders easier:

- Nouns which refer to masculine or feminine people will have the corresponding gender e.g. *der Großvater, die Mutter*
- Nouns which end in the following are usually masculine:
  -ant -er -ich -ig -ing -ismus -ist -or
- Nouns which end as follows are usually feminine:
  -e -heit -keit -ik -in -ion -schaft -ung
- Nouns which end in the following are usually neuter:
  -chen -lein -um
- Words from other languages are also often neuter e.g. *das Hotel*
- The gender of a compound noun is always the gender of the last noun element e.g. *das Taschengeld, die Zugkarte, der Hausmann*

1.2 Definite and indefinite articles

	masc.	fem.	neut.	plural	masc.	fem.	neut.	plural
nom.	*der*	*die*	*das*	*die*	*ein*	*eine*	*ein*	*keine*
acc.	*den*	*die*	*das*	*die*	*einen*	*eine*	*ein*	*keine*
gen.	*des*	*der*	*des*	*der*	*eines*	*einer*	*eines*	*keiner*
dat.	*dem*	*der*	*dem*	*den*	*einem*	*einer*	*einem*	*keinen*

- German has a distinctive use of articles and you should be careful in instances where German uses the article and English doesn't as well as other cases where English uses the article but German doesn't.
  Die Natur ist schön. Nature is beautiful.
  Sie ist Lehrerin. She is a teacher.

(1) Translate into German: I live in a house. She has a brother. The book is good.

2 Prepositions and cases

2.1 Cases

The German case system helps show how a sentence fits together.
- The nominative case is used for the subject of a sentence.
  ***Der Vater** hat immer Recht!* Father is always right!
  It is always used after verbs like ***sein, werden*** and ***bleiben.***

- The accusative case is used for the object of a sentence, in certain expressions of time and after certain prepositions: ***bis, durch, entlang, für, gegen, ohne, um***

  *Kauft er **den Hund?*** Is he buying the dog?
  *Sie joggt **durch den Wald.*** She jogs through the forest.
  ***Nächste Woche** fahre ich nach Italien.* I am going to Italy next week.

- The genitive case is used to show possession after certain prepositions:
außerhalb, innerhalb, statt, trotz, während, wegen

  Die Filme des Jahres.   Films of the year.
  Ich wohne außerhalb der Stadt.   I live outside the town.

- The dative case is used for the indirect object of a sentence after certain prepositions: *aus, außer, bei, dank, gegenüber, mit, nach, seit, von, zu*

  Ich gebe dem Hund einen Knochen.   I give the dog a bone.
  Heute gehe ich zum Arzt.   Today I am going to the doctor.

N.B. Contractions: *bei + dem = **beim**, von + dem = **vom**, zu + der = **zur**,*
*zu + dem = **zum***

2.2 Dual case prepositions

Nine prepositions take either the accusative case or the dative case: *an, auf, hinter, in, neben, über, unter, vor, zwischen*

When these prepositions indicate the position of a thing or an action, they are followed by the dative case:
Er arbeitet im Supermarkt.   He works in the supermarket.

When they indicate the direction of a movement, they are followed by the accusative case:
Er geht in den Supermarkt.   He is going into the supermarket.
N.B. Contractions: *an + dem = **am**, an + das = **ans**, in + dem = **im**,*
*in + das = **ins***

(2) Translate into German: He is a small man. I have no idea. He has no time for his son. We're staying at home because of the bad weather. Are you writing to the sister? They are walking in the forest. They are going into the park.

3 Adjectives and adverbs

3.1 Demonstrative and interrogative adjectives

Demonstrative adjectives include: *dieser* this *jener* that *jeder* each, every
There is only one interrogative adjective, used for questions: *welcher* which
All four words follow the same declension as the definite article:

	masc.	fem.	neut.	plural
nom.	*dieser*	*diese*	*dieses*	*diese*
acc.	*diesen*	*diese*	*dieses*	*diese*
gen.	*dieses*	*dieser*	*dieses*	*dieser*
dat.	*diesem*	*dieser*	*diesem*	*diesen*

(3) Translate into German: This girl is very clever. I like that idea.

3.2 Adjective endings

Adjectives after a noun do not add any endings but when an adjective is used before a noun it has particular endings depending on the case, gender and number of the noun.

Adjective endings after the definite article, **alle, dieser** etc:

	masc.	fem.	neut.	plural
nom.	e	e	e	en
acc.	en	e	e	en
gen.	en	en	en	en
dat.	en	en	en	en

Adjective endings after the indefinite article, **kein** and the possessive adjectives:

	masc.	fem.	neut.	plural
nom.	er	e	es	en
acc.	en	e	es	en
gen.	en	en	en	en
dat.	en	en	en	en

Adjectives used without an article or other defining word, e.g after a number:

	masc.	fem.	neut.	plural
nom.	er	e	es	e
acc.	en	e	es	e
gen.	en	er	en	er
dat.	em	er	em	en

(4) Translate into German: The boy is clever. I hate black coffee. I spoke to the pretty girl. He is wearing a black coat.

3.3 Adverbs

Adverbs describe **how** something is done – well, badly, efficiently. In English they usually end in '-ly' although there are exceptions such as 'well' and 'fast'.

- In German any adjective can be used as an adverb without alteration: *langsam* slowly
- There are adverbs of place describing the place where something happens: *hier* here
- Adverbs of time describe when something took place: *selten* rarely
- Adverbial phrases such as *mit Eile* quickly
- Interrogative adverbs ask where and when etc something happens: *wann* when

(5) Translate into German: He drove quickly. She smiled happily.

3.4 Comparison of adjectives

Comparatives are used to compare two things using the same adjective, while superlatives compare three or more things to each other again using the same adjective.

Comparatives are formed using the adjective, adding -er and adding the appropriate adjective ending: **klein** small **kleiner** smaller
When comparing two things **als** in German translates the English 'than'.

To form the superlative -**(e)s**t is added to the adjective, followed by the appropriate adjective ending: das **billigste** Auto   the cheapest car

Some adjectives add an umlaut when forming comparatives and superlatives, and some are irregular:

adjective	comparative	superlative
lang	*länger*	*(das) längste*
warm	*wärmer*	*(das) wärmste*
groß	*größer*	*(das) größte*
gesund	*gesünder*	*(das) gesündeste*
gut	*besser*	*(das) beste*
hoch	*höher*	*(das) höchste*
nah	*näher*	*(das) nächste*

6 Put a comparative adjective in each gap to complete the sentence:
Die Schule ist stressig aber die Arbeit ist noch _____.
Schokolade ist schlecht für die Gesundheit aber Fastfood ist noch_____.

3.5 Comparison of adverbs

These follow a very similar pattern to those of adjectives when forming comparatives and superlatives.

schnell	quickly	**schneller**	more quickly
einfach	easily	**einfacher**	more easily
am schnellsten	most quickly	**am einfachsten**	most easily

Irregular adverb comparisons:

adverb	comparative	superlative
gern	*lieber*	*am liebsten*
gut	*besser*	*am besten*
viel	*mehr*	*am meisten*
bald	*eher*	*am ehesten*

7 Wer sind _____, die Deutschen oder die Engländer?
(*friendlier*) Zum Frühstück essen die Engländer_____.
(*more healthily*)

4 Pronouns

4.1 Modes of address

There are three words for "you" in German:

du   for one person you know very well
ihr   for more than one person you know very well
Sie   for one or more people older than yourself, and people in authority

8 Translate into German "Are you coming to the cinema tonight?" using all three modes of address.

4.2 Personal pronouns

These alter according to case:

nom.	acc.	dat.	nom.	acc.	dat.
ich	mich	mir	wir	uns	uns
du	dich	dir	ihr	euch	euch
er	ihn	ihm	sie	sie	ihnen
sie	sie	ihr	Sie	Sie	Ihnen
es	es	ihm			

9 Fill the gaps with the correct pronouns: Gib _____ deine Hand. (*me*) Ich sehe _____ mindestens zweimal am Tag. (*her*) Ich kann _____ nicht finden. (*him*)

4.3 Reflexive pronouns

Reflexive pronouns are used with reflexive verbs to mean "myself" etc and are used in the accusative and dative cases as follows:

nom.	acc.	dat.	nom.	acc.	dat.
ich	mich	mir	wir	uns	uns
du	dich	dir	ihr	euch	euch
er/sie/es/man	sich	sich	sie	sich	sich
			Sie	sich	sich

10 Insert the appropriate reflexive pronoun: Wie oft duschst du ____ ____? Wo befindet _____ die nächste Post? Ich wasche ____ die Hände.

4.4 Relative pronouns

These mean 'who' or 'which/that' and they join simple sentences together. These exist for each gender and case:

	masc.	fem.	neut.	plural
nom.	der	die	das	die
acc.	den	die	das	die

gen.	dessen	deren	dessen	deren
dat.	dem	der	dem	denen

- The relative pronoun agrees in gender and number with the noun to which it refers.
- It takes its case from the role it plays within the relative clause.
- It must have a comma before it.
- It sends the verb to the end of the clause.
- It can be missed out in English but not in German.
- After *alles, viel, manches, nichts, allerlei* and the superlatives, the relative pronoun *was* is used instead.
- If the relative pronoun refers to the whole of the other clause, *was* is used again.

(11) Translate into German: The teacher who teaches Latin is funny. The café that sells good coffee is expensive.

4.5 Possessive pronouns

Possessive adjectives can be used as pronouns (without a noun) and the forms are the same as for possessive adjectives, except that the masculine ends in *-er* in the nominative, and the neuter nominative and accusative end in *-es*.

Possessive pronouns take their gender from the noun to which they refer and their case from the part they play in the clause or sentence, e.g nominative:

masc.	fem.	neuter	plural
meiner	meine	meines	meine
ihrer	ihre	ihres	ihre

(12) Translate into German: My house is bigger than yours. My garden is smaller than yours.

4.6 Indefinite pronouns

These stand in place of nouns, but don't refer to anything definite (someone, no-one):
jemand someone *niemand* no-one *einer* one *keiner* no-one
jeder each *man* one *etwas* something *nichts* nothing

jemand and *niemand* add *-en* in the accusative and *-em* in the dative while *einer, keiner* and *jeder* decline like *dieser* (3.2).
man is widely used in German but only in the nominative.
etwas and *nichts* do not change whatever case they are in.

(13) Translate into German: nothing good, something interesting, no-one knows

4.7 Interrogative pronouns

The interrogative pronoun *wer* refers to people and declines as follows:

nom.	*wer*	**acc.**	*wen*	**gen.**	*wessen*	**dat.**	*wem*

When referring to things, German uses:

nom.	*was*		**gen.**	*wessen*
acc.	*was* or *wo-/wor-* + *preposition* e.g. *wodurch/woran*		**dat.**	*wo/wor-* + *preposition* e.g. *womit/worauf*

(14) Fill in the gaps: _____ist das? _____ hast du im Kino gesehen?

5 Verbs – the basics

5.1 Reflexive verbs

Reflexive verbs are used with the reflexive pronouns (4.3). Many verbs are reflexive in German but not in English: ***sich waschen***   to have a wash

Many reflexive verbs are to do with actions done to yourself, but this need not be the case: ***sich etwas überlegen***   to consider something

Reflexive verbs normally take the accusative pronoun but they can use the dative pronoun if there is another direct object in the sentence.
acc: *ich wasche mich*   dat: *ich bürste mir die Haare*

5.2 Impersonal verbs and verbs with a dative object

Some verbs are often used with *es* as an indefinite subject.

Gefällt es dir hier?	Do you like it here?
Es gibt ...	there is/ there are
Es kommt darauf an ...	It depends on ...
Es geht ihm gut.	He is well.
Hat es geschmeckt?	Did you enjoy it? (food)
Es tut mir leid.	I am sorry.
Es ist mir kalt.	I am cold.
Es gelingt ihm, ... zu + inf.	He succeeds in ...ing

Many idiomatic verbs take a dative object (4.2).

Es fehlt mir sehr.	I really miss it.
Das Bein tut mir weh.	My leg hurts.
Das Kleid steht Ihnen gut.	The dress suits you.
Die Hose passt ihm nicht.	The trousers don't fit him.
Das Buch gehört meiner Mutter.	The book belongs to my mother.
Das Bild gefällt ihm.	He likes the picture.

5.3 Separable and inseparable verbs

There are a few prefixes in German which are inseparable and cannot be split from the verb: ***be- ent- ge- ver- emp- er- miss- zer-***
The stress in these verbs is in on the second syllable.

Most other prefixes are separable and go to the end of the clause or sentence. In the infinitive the prefix is stressed.

A few prefixes are separable in some verbs and not in others.

durch　　*um*　　　*unter*　　*wider*　　*über*　　*wieder*

5.4 Modal verbs

German has six modal verbs. They work with the infinitive of another verb which goes to the end of the sentence.

dürfen	to be allowed to	**müssen**	to have to
können	to be able to	**sollen**	to be supposed to
mögen	to like	**wollen**	to want to

6　The main tenses

6.1 The present tense

The present tense in German has three translations in English. It describes actions which are happening in the present, actions which are happening now on a regular basis as well as actions which will happen in the near future.

wissen, the auxiliary verbs and the modal verbs are very irregular and need to be learned separately:

wissen	*sein*	*haben*	*werden*
ich weiß	*ich bin*	*ich habe*	*ich werde*
du weißt	*du bist*	*du hast*	*du wirst*
er/sie weiß	*er/sie ist*	*er/sie hat*	*er/sie wird*
wir wissen	*wir sind*	*wir haben*	*wir werden*
ihr wisst	*ihr seid*	*ihr habt*	*ihr werdet*
sie/Sie wissen	*sie/Sie sind*	*sie/Sie haben*	*sie/Sie werden*

dürfen	*können*	*mögen*	*müssen*	*sollen*	*wollen*
ich darf	*ich kann*	*ich mag*	*ich muss*	*ich soll*	*ich will*
du darfst	*du kannst*	*du magst*	*du musst*	*du sollst*	*du willst*
er/sie darf	*er/sie kann*	*er/sie mag*	*er/sie musst*	*er soll*	*er/sie will*
wir dürfen	*wir können*	*wir mögen*	*wir müssen*	*wir sollen*	*wir wollen*
ihr dürft	*ihr könnt*	*ihr mögt*	*ihr müsst*	*ihr sollt*	*ihr wollt*
sie/Sie dürfen	*sie/Sie können*	*sie/Sie mögen*	*sie/Sie müssen*	*sie/Sie sollen*	*sie/Sie wollen*

6.2 The perfect tense

The perfect tense in German is used in speech to describe actions which happened in the past. It can be translated by the English simple past (I did) or by the English perfect tense (I have done).

Most verbs form their perfect tense with the present tense of the auxiliary verb *haben* and a past participle. *haben* takes the normal verb position, while the past participle goes to the end of the clause or the sentence.

- weak verbs form their past participle from the normal verb stem with the prefix *ge-* and the ending *-t* (***gemacht, gekauft***)
- mixed verbs and modal verbs change the stem but the prefix endings remain the same (***bringen – gebracht , denken – ge***dacht)
- the past participle of strong verbs often have a changed stem, and take the ***ge-*** prefix and an ***-en*** ending (*gegessen, gesungen, getrunken*)
- the past participle of the auxiliaries are as follows:
  sein   **gewesen**   *haben*   **gehabt**   *werden*   **geworden**
- verbs with separable prefixes insert *ge-* after the prefix (*eingekauft, aufgeschrieben, nachgedacht*) and verbs with inseparable prefixes do not use the *ge* at all (***bekommen, erreicht, missverstanden, verbracht***)

Certain verbs, which have no object, use the auxiliary verb ***sein*** to form the perfect tense. The majority of these verbs are strong/irregular verbs.

- Verbs of motion: *gehen*   *fahren*   *aufstehen*
- Verbs expressing a change in state or emotion:
  aufwachen   *werden*   *wachsen*   *einschlafen*
- Other verbs: *bleiben*   *sein*

The past participles of modal verbs are as follows:
dürfen   **gedurft**   *müssen*   **gemusst**   *können*   **gekonnt**
sollen   **gesollt**   *mögen*   **gemocht**   *wollen*   **gewollt**
But when a modal verb is used with another verb in the infinitive, the perfect tense is formed with the infinitive of the modal verb rather than the past participle. ***Sehen, hören*** and ***lassen*** behave like modal verbs and use the infinitive in the perfect tense.

6.3 The imperfect tense

German uses the imperfect tense to describe past events in writing for narrative, reports and accounts. Regular/weak verbs form the imperfect tense by adding certain endings to the stem of the verb:

*ich spiel**te**, wir spiel**ten**, du spiel**test**, ihr spiel**tet**, er/sie spiel**te**, sie/Sie spiel**ten***
If the stem of the verb ends in *-t* or several consonants an extra *e* is added: ***arbeitete, trocknete.***
Strong verbs form this tense by changing the stem and these verbs need to be learned individually. They also add these endings:

ich	no ending	wir	*-en*
du	*-st*	*ihr*	*-t*
er/sie	no ending *sie/Sie*		*-en*

e.g. *gehen – ich ging, trinken – ich trank, lesen – ich las*

Mixed verbs change their stem as strong verbs do but add the weak verb endings: *bringen – ich brachte, nennen – ich nannte, denken – ich dachte*

Modal verbs work like mixed verbs in that they add the same endings as weak verbs but mostly change the stem:
dürfen – ich durfte, müssen – ich musste, können – ich konnte, sollen – ich sollte, mögen – ich mochte, wollen – ich wollte

The auxiliary verbs in the imperfect tense:

sein	*haben*	*werden*
ich war	*ich hatte*	*ich wurde*
du warst	*du hattest*	*du wurdest*
er/sie war	*er/sie hatte*	*er/sie wurde*
wir waren	*wir hatten*	*wir wurden*
ihr wart	*ihr hattet*	*ihr wurdet*
sie/Sie waren	*sie/Sie hatten*	*sie/Sie wurden*

6.4 The pluperfect tense

The pluperfect tense is used to express something that had happened before something else. It is formed by combining the imperfect tense of the auxiliary verb with the past participle.
sprechen – ich hatte gesprochen
fahren – ich war gefahren

6.5 The future tense

The present tense is often used to describe an event which will happen in the near future especially if there is an expression of time indicating future meaning. *Morgen gehe ich nach Hause.* I am going home tomorrow.

The future tense is more precise and gives emphasis to the future aspect of a statement. The future tense is formed from the present tense of **werden** plus the infinitive, which goes to the end of the sentence.
Nächstes Jahr werde ich nach Indien fahren. I am going to India next year.

(15) Translate into German: **I get up.** *(present)* **We flew to Zurich.** *(perfect)* **We were quite poor.** *(imperfect)* **I had received a book.** *(pluperfect)* **We will go to university.** *(future)*

7 Conjunctions and word order

7.1 Word order in main clauses

The verb in German must always be the second idea in a main clause. Any phrase describing time, manner or place can begin a sentence but the verb must still remain in second place followed by the subject. Phrases have to be arranged in the order Time-Manner-Place, even if only two of the three phrases are used in a sentence.

7.2. Negative sentences

The negative adverbs **nicht** and **nie** go as close as possible to the end of the sentence but before adjectives, phrases of manner, phrases of place, infinitives, past participles and separable prefixes. **nicht** can also go before words where a special emphasis is necessary.

7.3 Questions

Questions in German are mostly expressed by inversion (swapping the subject with the verb). This inversion also happens with question words. In an **indirect question** the verb goes to the end of the clause.

7.4 Conjunctions

These co-ordinating conjunctions **do not** change the word order when connecting two clauses: *aber, denn, oder, sondern, und.*
sondern is usually used after a negative statement.
aber is used to express 'on the other hand'.

There are a large number of subordinating conjunctions which send the verb to the end of the clause: *als, als ob, (an)statt, bevor, bis, da, damit, dass, falls, nachdem, ob, obgleich, obwohl, seit(dem), sobald, sodass, solange, während, wenn, wie*

Some adverbs are used to link sentences together and the verb which follows inverts as normal. These are: *also, darum, deshalb, deswegen, folglich, und so*

7.5 Relative clauses

Relative clauses are subordinate clauses introduced by a relative pronoun. The verb in such a clause is sent to the end of the clause and the relative clause also has commas at each end to separate it from the end of the sentence.
Das Schloss, dass wir gestern besuchten, war sehr schön. The castle we visited yesterday was very beautiful.

(16) Put these words into the correct order to form sentences:
mit meinem Freund-nach Italien-letzten Sommer ich bin gefahren-mit dem Zug.
entscheiden sich-Mütter-viele Frauen-für eine Teilzeitarbeit-einmal-sie-werden.

b, d und g CD Track 6

Vergleichen Sie:

Bild	*o**b***
bleiben	*schreib**t***
Deutsch	*gesun**d***
dürfen	*bal**d***
gut	*Ta**g***
ganz	*Erfol**g***

Consonants *b*, *d* and *g* are pronounced like *p*, *k* and *t* respectively when they appear at the end of a word or in front of *s* or *t*.

Üben Sie jetzt diese Sätze:

Jeden Tag gesund essen – der gute Weg zum Erfolg!
Mein deutscher Freund wird bald kommen.
Ich weiß nicht, ob er lange bleibt.

-ig, -ich, -isch CD Track 7

Wiederholen Sie die Adjektive:

wenig	*möglich*	*praktisch*
billig	*eigentlich*	*politisch*
witzig	*jugendlich*	*launisch*
günstig	*schriftlich*	*erfinderisch*

Versuchen Sie jetzt diesen Zungenbrecher:

Theoretisch ist das richtig, aber eigentlich gar nicht wichtig – beschwichtigt der ewig praktische Herr Derwisch.

s, ß, st, sp CD Track 8

Üben Sie diese Wörter:

Sonntag	*sein*
Stein	*Straße*
Fußball	*Spaß*
Sorge	*Pass*
Staatsangehörigkeit	*Statistik*

Zungenbrecher:

Am Sonntag sitzt sein Sohn auf der Straße in der Stadt, sonst strickt er Socken, spielt Fußball und sammelt Steine.

Pronunciation

ei, ie CD Track 9

Wiederholen Sie:

eins, zwei, drei
Eintracht und Zwietracht
Dienstag, Mittwoch und Freitag
schwierig
der Schweiß

Die Arbeit ist nicht schwierig, aber schweißtreibend.
Ich schreibe. Ich schrieb. Ich habe geschrieben.
Er muss sich entscheiden. Er hat sich entschieden.
Liebeslieder von Liebe und Leiden

Lange und kurze Vokale CD Track 10

Wiederholen Sie:

langer Vokal:
mag, Rad, Spaß, Abend, sagen
sehr, gehen, jedes, Federball, Meter
mir, hier, Spiel, Ziel, viel
ohne, wohnen, so, oder, Mode
Ruhe, Schule, Fuß, zu, nun

kurzer Vokal:
hallo, etwas, Geschmack, Stadt, satt
Essen, Tennis, schlecht, Welt, Geld
bist, sich, immer, finden, Wirkung
kommen, besonders, Kosten, gebrochen, noch
muss, Mutter, Eiskunstlauf, Druck, Schuss

Vokale mit Umlaut CD Track 11

Wiederholen Sie:

schön	*erhöht*	*gewöhnlich*	*könnte*
über	*hübsch*	*Grüße*	*müsste*
Ähnlichkeit	*erwähnen*	*Fähigkeit*	*ändern*

Lesen Sie diese Wörter laut. Überprüfen Sie danach die Aussprache.

übertrieben   Aufklärungsarbeit   hören   jeder fünfte   Gegensätze
möglich   Gefühl   Schönheitsideal   schädlich   fünf
Essstörungen   gefährlich   Öffentlichkeit   übermäßig   abhängig

Zungenbrecher:

Der Mondschein schien schon schön.

-z und -zw

Wiederholen Sie:

Ziel	Zug	Zaun	Zweig	Zwerg	Zweck
Einzelzimmer	jetzt	zuletzt	kurz	nützlich	
Unterstützung	Sturz	Arzt	zwanzig	gezwungen	zwölf

Hören Sie zu und wiederholen Sie:

jetzt – zuletzt
zu zweit – Zeit
kurz – Sturz
zwanzig – Zwetschgen
Zweck – Zecke

Probieren Sie diese Sätze:

Setzen Sie sich in den Zug.
Zwischen zwölf und zwei.
Zieh jetzt kurz am Seil.
Zwei Ziegen sitzen vor dem Zaun.

Zungenbrecher:

Zwischen zwei Zelten zwitschern zwölf Zaunkönige.

Compound words

Wiederholen Sie:

a gleich/geschlechtliche Partnerschaften
b Lebens/abschnitts/gefährte
c Wieder/heirat
d Geschäfts/reise
e auseinander/brechen
f Kinder/tages/stätte
g Wieder/vereinigung
h Gehirn/masse
i Wohn/gemeinschaft
j Abenteuer/lust

Vocabulary

Vocabulary learning tips

▶ Record vocabulary accurately – colour coding for genders is a very useful tool, e.g. write all masculine words in red, feminine in blue and neuter in black.

▶ Store all vocabulary in the same place. Organise a system that works for you early on. Set aside some time every week to record new vocabulary learned. Perhaps record vocabulary by topic area.

▶ Spend a few minutes every day learning vocabulary. Little and often is the key to successful vocabulary learning.

▶ Use the 'look, cover, write and check' method.

▶ Learn vocabulary from English into German as well as from German to English.

▶ Try using index cards with German on one side and English on the other and test yourself on a regular basis.

▶ Ask someone else to test you, especially out of sequence.

▶ Try to learn chunks of language in context.

▶ Group words together by writing lists of synonyms or opposites e.g. lieben/hassen, die Ehe/die Scheidung.

▶ List words in families: from the verb can you find nouns and adjectives which relate to it?

e.g	lieben	die Liebe	beliebt
	hassen	der Hass	hässlich

▶ Write out a set of words in jumbled form, then come back later and try to unjumble them. Can you sort out these eight words on the topic of smoking and drinking?

cehnaru	lakhool	ühctgis	hggiänba
maluq	boetnrev	renettgaiz	kbata

(rauchen, Alkohol, süchtig, abhängig, Qualm, verboten, Zigaretten, Tabak)

▶ Write out words with gaps for missing letters or sentences and try to complete them later. Complete these words linked to media.

Fe-nse-en   s-rfe-   -erb-ng   -edi-n   -eit-ng Z-it-chrift

(Fernsehen, surfen, Werbung, Medien, Zeitung, Zeitschrift)

General vocabulary

Time phrases

ab und zu	*now and again*
danach	*after that*
davor	*before that*
häufig	*often*
kaum	*rarely*
nach wie vor	*still*

Useful phrases

allerdings	*mind you*
alles in allem	*all in all*
als je zuvor	*than ever before*
andererseits	*on the other hand*
auf keinen Fall	*on no account*
drittens	*thirdly*
einerseits	*on the one hand*
erstens	*firstly*
hauptsächlich	*mainly*
heutzutage	*nowadays*
im Allgemeinen	*in general*
im Durchschnitt	*on average*
im Gegensatz zu	*as opposed to*
im Grunde	*basically*
im Vergleich zu	*compared with*
in der Tat	*in fact*
jedenfalls	*in any case*
keineswegs	*on no account*
möglicherweise	*possibly*
offenbar	*apparently*
ohnenhin	*anyway*
schließlich	*finally*
selbstverständlich	*obviously*
übrigens	*by the way*
umgekehrt	*vice versa*
vergeblich	*in vain*
vermutlich	*presumably*
vor allem	*above all*
wesentlich	*considerably, essentially*
zusätzlich	*additionally*
zweitens	*secondly*

Presentations

Abschließend kann man sagen, dass ...	*To sum up, one can say that ...*
Einerseits ... andererseits ...	*On the one hand ... on the other ...*

Vocabulary

Es handelt sich um ...	*It is a question of ...*
Es heißt, dass ...	*It is said that ...*
Es fragt sich, ob ...	*The question is whether ...*
Im nächsten Punkt geht es um ...	*The next point deals with ...*
In diesem Kurzreferat geht es um das Thema ...	*The theme of this short speech is ...*
In diesem Kurzreferat möchte ich über ... sprechen.	*In this short speech I would like to talk about ...*
Man sieht, dass ...	*One can see that ...*
Statistiken zeigen, dass ...	*Statistics show that ...*
Zuerst spreche ich über ...	*First I will speak about ...*

Opinions

ich behaupte, dass ...	*I claim that ...*
ich bezweifle, dass ...	*I doubt that ...*
ich bin der Meinung, dass ...	*I think that ...*
ich bin total dagegen	*I am completely against it*
ich bin überzeugt, dass ...	*I am convinced that ...*
ich finde, dass ...	*I find that ...*
ich gebe zu, dass ...	*I admit that ...*
ich glaube, dass ...	*I believe that ...*
ich glaube nicht unbedingt, dass ...	*I don't necessarily believe that ...*
ich habe den Eindruck, dass ...	*I have the impression that ...*
ich habe erfahren, dass ...	*I have learnt that ...*
ich hoffe, dass ...	*I hope that ...*
ich interessiere mich (nicht) für ...	*I am (not) interested in ...*
ich mache mir Sorgen um...	*I am concerned about ...*
ich meine, dass ...	*I think that ...*
ich nehme an, dass ...	*I assume that ...*
ich schlage vor, dass ...	*I suggest that ...*
ich stimme zu, dass ...	*I agree that ...*
ich vermute, dass ...	*I suspect that ...*
die Vorteile/Nachteile sind ...	*the advantages/disadvantages are ...*
meiner Ansicht nach ...	*in my opinion ...*
meiner Meinung nach ...	*in my opinion ...*
meines Erachtens ...	*in my opinion ...*

Arguments

das beweist, dass ...	*that proves that ...*
das ist der Grund warum ...	*that is the reason why ...*
es betrifft ...	*it concerns ...*
es freut mich, dass ...	*I am pleased that ...*
es geht um ...	*it's about ...*

es handelt sich um ...	*it's about ...*
es ist fraglich, ob ...	*it's questionable whether ...*
es ist klar, dass ...	*it's clear that ...*
es ist nicht wahr, dass ...	*it's not true that ...*
es ist nicht zu glauben, dass ...	*it's not to be believed that ...*
es ist die Rede von ...	*there's talk of ...*
es kann sein, dass ...	*it can be that ...*
es kommt darauf an, was ...	*it depends on what ...*
es steht fest, dass ...	*one thing is for sure and that is ...*
es stellt sich heraus, dass ...	*it turns out that ...*
es stimmt nicht, dass ...	*it's not true that ...*
ich stimme dir (nicht) zu	*I (don't) agree with you*
im Gegenteil	*on the contrary*

Topic vocabulary

Unit 1 Medien

die Sendung	*programme*
das Programm	*channel*
das Fernsehgerät	*television set*
sich entspannen	*to relax*
das Fernsehen	*television (concept)*
der Fernseher	*television set*
das Kabelfernsehen	*cable television*
gesättigt	*saturated*
die Gewalt	*violence*
die Kriminalität	*crime*
verherrlichen	*to glorify*
die Tatsache	*fact*
darstellen	*to portray*
verharmlosen	*to play down*
verringern	*to reduce*
die Werbung	*advertising*
beeinflussen	*to influence*
verbieten	*to forbid, to ban*
verführen	*to seduce*
der Konsumzwang	*pressure to buy*
die Gehirnwäsche	*brainwashing*
unentbehrlich	*indispensable*
verfestigen	*to reinforce*
der Werbespot	*advert*
die Boulevardzeitung	*tabloid newspaper*
objektiv	*objective*
die Sensationsmache	*sensationalism*

ausführlich	*detailed*
subjektiv	*subjective*
der Kommentar	*commentary*
der Klatsch	*gossip, scandal*
der Tratsch	*tittle-tattle*
der Zeugenbericht	*eye-witness report*
tagtäglich	*daily*
empfangen	*to receive*
die Glotze	*'the box' (slang for TV)*
rund um die Uhr	*around the clock*
der Zuschauer	*viewer*
herunterladen	*download*
gesättigt	*saturated*
die Qualität des Angebots	*the quality of what's on offer*
die Staffel	*round, or series*
ausbeuten	*to exploit*
erfinderisch	*imaginative*
wahllos	*indiscriminately*
erstrebenswert	*desirable*
aufmerksam machen auf (+ Akk.)	*to make aware of*
missbrauchen	*to abuse*
berichten	*to report*
veröffentlichen	*to publish*
einschränken	*to restrict*
äußern	*to express*
ausstrahlen	*to broadcast*

Unit 2 Die Welt der Kommunikation

das Handy	*mobile phone*
die Handygebühren (pl.)	*mobile phone charges*
das Telefonat	*phone call*
SMS schicken	*to send text messages/to text*
der Internetanschluss	*internet connection*
herunterladen	*to download*
aufnehmen	*to record*
speichern	*to store*
der Bildschirm	*screen*
auftauchen	*to pop up*
der Zugang	*access*
die Recherchen (pl.)	*research*
aufladen	*to upload*
Zensur einführen	*to censor*

Unit 3 Freizeit

faulenzen	*to laze around*
Werken (pl.)	*handicrafts*
saisonbedingt	*seasonal*
die Kulturveranstaltung	*cultural event*
synchronisiert	*dubbed*
die Leinwand	*screen*
der Stummfilm	*silent film*
unterhaltend	*entertaining*
der Inhalt	*content*
der Darsteller	*performer*
der Untertitel	*subtitle*
die Vorführung	*performance*
ausländisch	*foreign*
die Kammermusik	*chamber music*
die Fotografie	*photography*
der Dichter	*poet*
der Schriftsteller	*writer*
das Gemälde	*painting*
die Skulptur	*sculpture*
der Denkmal/die Denkmäler	*monument(s)*
die Poesie	*poetry*
der Roman	*novel*
die Ausstellung	*exhibition*
der Maler	*painter*
das Oper	*opera*
das Weltkulturerbe	*world cultural inheritance*
der Dirigent	*conductor*
die Uraufführung	*premiere*

Unit 4 Die Jugend

meine Kultur bewahren	*to retain my culture*
nahe bei meiner Familie leben	*to live near my family*
selbstständig seine Karriere machen	*to make one's career independently*
Symbole unserer Identität	*signs of our identity*
keine richtigen Freunde	*not true friends*
die Marke	*label*
werden gezwungen	*are forced*
anders aussehen	*to look different*
ein Teil meiner Identität	*part of my identity*
aus religiösen Gründen	*for religious reasons*
die Gesellschaft	*society*
das Verständnis	*understanding*
die Minderheit	*minority*

Vocabulary

das Verhalten	behaviour
die Menschenrechte (pl.)	human rights
behindert	disabled
obdachlos	homeless
empfindlich	sensitive
gelähmt	disabled
pingelig	fussy

Unit 5 Sport

die Sportart	type of sport
der Cholesterinwert	cholesterol level
das Immunsystem	immune system
das Herz	heart
die Fertiggerichte (pl.)	ready meals
der Schlaganfall	stroke
der Trendsport	fashionable sports
der Breitensport	mass sport
selbst Schuld sein	to be one's own fault
die Bewegung	movement
fördern	to promote
der Stoffwechsel	metabolism
der Kreislauf	circulation
der Mangel an	lack of
ausgewogen	balanced
die Empfehlung	recommendation
die Flüssigkeit	fluid
vorbeugen	to prevent
die Belastung	pressure, strain
die einzelnen Teams	individual teams
das Durchhaltevermögen	perseverance
der Teufelskreis	vicious circle

Unit 6 Gesundheit

der Qualm	smoke
infiziert	infected
beliebt	beloved
die Überdosis	overdose
erlauben	to allow
bewusstlos	unconscious
missbrauchen	to abuse
das Rauchen	smoking
schädigen	to damage
der Blutalkoholspiegel	blood-alcohol level
die Droge	drug

das Rauschgift	*drug*
sich spritzen	*to inject oneself*
süchtig	*addicted*
der Mut	*courage*
der Kettenraucher	*chain smoker*
das Selbstwertgefühl	*self esteem*
die Sucht	*addiction*
die Magersucht	*anorexia*
die Essstörung	*eating disorder*
der Anoretiker	*anorexic (noun)*
das Körpergewicht	*body weight*
das Abnehmen	*weight loss*
das Unterbewusstsein	*subconscious*
verstärken	*to strengthen*
verdrängen	*to repress*
die Ernährung	*nourishment, food, diet*
häufig	*common*
nachlassen	*to neglect*
versagen	*to refuse, deny*
die Ursache	*cause*
vermeiden	*to avoid*

Unit 7 Tourismus

der Urlaub	*holiday*
die Ferien (pl.)	*holidays*
die Ruhe	*rest*
die Entspannung	*relaxation*
die Erholung	*recovery*
sich gönnen	*to allow oneself*
das Bruttoinlandsprodukt	*gross domestic product*
die Nachfrage	*demand*
die Wirtschaft	*economy*
steigen	*to rise*
zunehmen	*to increase*
die Treibhausgasemissionen (pl.)	*greenhouse gas emissions*
der Gemeinschaftssinn	*sense of community*
umweltfreundlich	*environmentally friendly*
der Arbeitsplatz	*employment*
der Wohlstand	*affluence*
zerstören	*to destroy*
die Reisehäufigkeit	*frequency of travel*
die Nachfrage	*demand*
sich bemühen	*to try hard*
schützen	*to protect*

erhalten	*to keep*
die Schadstoffe (pl.)	*harmful substances*
der Schwefelgehalt	*sulphur content*
belasten	*to pollute*
die Schienen (pl.)	*rail tracks*
das Verkehrsmittel	*transport*
die Besteuerung	*tax*
der Klimawandel	*climate change*

Unit 8 Familie

die Ehe	*marriage*
die Kita (Kindertagesstätte)	*nursery*
auseinander brechen	*to break up*
erziehen (erzog, erzogen)	*to raise*
allein erziehende Mutter	*single mother*
die tödliche Krankheit	*terminal illness*
die Stiefgeschwister (pl.)	*step-siblings*
Lehrling werden	*to become an apprentice*
die Wiederheirat	*remarriage*
geschiedene Eltern	*divorced parents*
das Nesthäkchen	*the youngest of the family*
schwanger sein	*to be pregnant*
strahlend	*sparkling*
der Druck	*pressure*
die Zuverlässigkeit	*reliability*
der Sinn für Humor	*sense of humour*
jede Menge Zeit für andere	*time for others*
gegenseitige Hilfe	*mutual help*
der Geschmack	*taste*
das Vertrauen	*trust*
die Großzügigkeit	*generosity*
die Abenteuerlust	*lust for adventure*
ähnliche Hobbys	*similar hobbies*
gemeinsamer Spaß	*fun together*
zuhören können	*to be able to listen*
die Sippe	*clan*
die Geborgenheit	*sense of belonging*
die kirchliche Trauung	*church wedding*
das Brautkleid	*wedding dress*
die Freiheit	*freedom*
gleichgeschlechtlich	*same sex*
die Scheidung	*divorce*
der Nachwuchs	*offspring*
vernachlässigen	*to neglect*

| die Rente | state pension |
| die Pension | pension from employment |

Unit 9 Schule und Ausbildung

das Abitur	A Level (equivalent)
sitzen bleiben	to repeat a year
die Grundschule	primary school
die Hauptschule	secondary school (years 5–9)
das Gymnasium	grammar school
die Realschule	secondary school (years 5–10)
die Gesamtschule	comprehensive school
das Internat(e)	boarding school
bestehen	to pass
durchfallen	to fail
die Klassenarbeit	(written) test
die Prüfung(en)	exam
das Zeugnis(se)	report
der Numerus clausus	very high marks
der Leistungskurs	main subject
der Kindergarten	nursery school
die Gleichberechtigung	equal opportunities
pauken	to swot, cram
beitragen zu	to contribute to
unter Druck	under pressure
das Selbstbewusstsein	self confidence
der Betrieb	business, factory
die Berufsausbildung	vocational training
das Bafög	student grant
(**B**undes**a**usbildungs**för**derung**s**gesetz)	
die Gebühren (pl.)	fees
benachteiligt	disadvantaged
verlangen	to request
klagen	to complain
der Durchschnitt	average
das Vorstellungsgespräch	interview
die Minderwertigkeitsgefühle (pl.)	feelings of low self esteem
sich bewerben	to apply for
unterstützen	to support
verzichten auf	to do without
der Erziehungsurlaub	career break (to look after children)
die Berufsaussichten (pl.)	career prospects

Transcript 1

1. Vanessa's parents are divorced and she lives with her mother and brother. Her father has not been in contact for years, but suddenly wants to see them.
2. Mother thinks she ought to give him a chance, but it is her decision.
3. Lukas' mother treats him like a child. She does not believe him.
4. Anxious/nervous and suspicious.
5. Father is very critical of her and makes fun of her in front of the whole family and in front of strangers.
6. She has not much self-confidence, and her marks in school are getting worse.

Transcript 2

1. J   2. M   3. P   4. J   5. M   6. P

Transcript 3

1. b   2. c   3. a   4. b

Transcript 4

1. als Ärztin/im Bereich Helfen (1)
2. eine gute Ausbildung, (1) Computer- (1) und Sprachkenntnisse (1)
3. Kommunikationsfähigkeiten, (1) Flexibilität (1) und Teamfähigkeiten (1)

Text 1

1. R   2. F   3. F   4. NT   5. R   6. F

Text 2

1. Man muss den Lebensstil ändern, damit das Leben gesünder wird.
2. Wenn die Ernährung ausgeglichen ist und viele Vitamine enthält, kann sie den Cholesterinspiegel reduzieren und vor Herzinfarkt schützen.
3. Man versucht, immer mehr am Tag zu schaffen, ohne sich genug Zeit dafür zu nehmen.
4. Man kann sich entspannen, indem man Yoga oder Meditation macht.
5. ‚Stopping' hilft zu erkennen, was im Leben wirklich wichtig ist.

Text 3

1. entstand   2. lernte … kennen   3. sparen   4. finden
5. herunterlädt   6. nachprüft

Text 4

Teil / Kategorien / abgeräumt / kann / erwartet / Füße